The High-Heel Footprint

The High-Heel Footprint ™

A Woman-ifesto
by
Dr. Mona Armijo

Mo-MindLab Press ©

2018 Dr. Mona Armijo: All rights reserved.

No part of this publication in print or in electronic format may be reproduced, stored in a retrieval system, or transmitted in any form or by any means, electronic, mechanical, photocopying, recording, or otherwise without the prior written permission of the publisher/author.

The contents of this book are provided for informational use only. It is subject to change without notice, and should not be construed as a commitment by Mo-MindLab Press. Mo-MindLab assumes no responsibility for any errors or inaccuracies that may appear in this book. The advice and strategies contained herein may not be suitable for your situation. You should consult with a professional where appropriate. The author shall not be liable for any loss or profit, mental health or other damages consequential or otherwise. The views expressed in this book do not necessarily reflect those of any agency or institution.

The High-Heel Footprint is a registered trademark of Dr. Mo - Strategy Consulting and Mind Lab.

Published in the United States by Mo-MindLab Press ©
First Edition.
ISBN-13: 978-0692190074
ISBN-10: 0692190074

Dedication

With faith and commitment, all things are possible. This book is dedicated to my three children who are the loves of my life - Tahnie, Joshua, and Bradley. In my quest for having a balanced life, my endless weekends and weeknights of studying, working at my home consulting business, and putting on my Mom hat was to bring you a better life. I hope I taught you to make a positive impact in the world, and have served as a role model for you to reach for your stars.

To all women, especially my amazing and supportive women friends (you know who you are)! The High-Heel Footprint is a concept I created with the intentions of amplifying YOU - to help you get your heel unstuck. It happens to all of us from time to time. Look deep inside your soul and bring out your wonderful woman. This book is an extension of my 2008/2009 doctoral dissertation research on women, with the purpose of sharing my ongoing research related to the challenges women continue to experience on a global scale.

To everyone (including the honorable men in the world), wake up each morning and step into your favorite shoes to seize your day! Step into your greatness and conquer your goals, with the purpose of serving others for the greater good of humanity. Continue to seek wisdom from life on a daily basis because learning and serving others, including yourself, is an endless journey.

Thank you to my proofreaders and editors, Valerie Brooks, Sandra Lopez Ovalle, Jennifer Honaker, and John Brand.

I am grateful to my siblings Bob, Dan, Ray Jr., Lenore and Suzette who give me nothing but love; and to my amazing parents Ray and Ida, who have passed into the light. They taught me humility and confidence. This book, however, is mostly in honor of the women who have blazed trails before me, so that I may have a better life. I vie to lift others up in my quest for leaving my High-Heel Footprint to better serve humanity. My greatest appreciation is to God and to my Master Spirits who inspire me daily as they guide me toward my purpose.

Contents

DEDICATION ii

CONTENTS v

INTRODUCTION vii

CHAPTER 1: THE HIGH-HEEL FOOTPRINT 1

CHAPTER 2: IT'S A PROBLEM 27

CHAPTER 3: STRATEGIES FOR THE PERSONAL EVOLUTION OF YOUR FOOTPRINT 55

CHAPTER 4: STRATEGIES FOR ORGANIZATIONS TO EVOLVE THE HIGH-HEEL FOOTPRINT 87

CHAPTER 5: THE WAY FORWARD 97

ABOUT THE AUTHOR 101

REFERENCES 103

Introduction

The High-Heel Footprint must evolve faster, and smarter. Enough of just being part of the status quo. Enough of "those" women not amplifying other women. Enough of the male ego being intimidated by the strong, smart woman. Misogyny must not be tolerated. Enough of "it's okay"—because it is "not" okay anymore. It never was.

"My mother told me to be a lady. For her, that meant be your own person, be independent."
Hon. Ruth Bader Ginsburg

"Don't mistake politeness for lack of strength."
Hon. Sonia Sotomayor

"Take criticism seriously, but not personally. If there is truth or merit in the criticism, try to learn from it. Otherwise, let it roll right off you." Hillary Clinton

You can waste your lives drawing lines, or you can live your life crossing them" Shonda Rhimes

"My brain, I believe, is the most beautiful part of my body."
Shakira

"We do not need magic to change the world. We carry all the power we need inside ourselves already: We have the power to imagine better."
J.K. Rowling

"Do not allow people to dim your shine because they are blinded. Tell them to put on some sunglasses, cuz we were born this way bitch!"
Lady Gaga

"There are two kinds of people, those who do the work and those who take the credit. Try to be in the first group;
there is less competition there."
Indira Gandhi

"If you're someone people count on, particularly in difficult moments, that's a sign of a life lived honorably." Rachel Maddow

"Every minute is a chance to change the world." Dolores Huerta

"When the whole world is silent, even one voice becomes powerful." Malala Yousafzai

"Doing the best at this moment, puts you in the best place for the next moment." Oprah Winfrey

"Define Your High-Heel Footprint: Find Your Purpose."
Dr. Mona Armijo

Why this book now? Because the time is *now*! What better time are you waiting for? This book is a collection of insights regarding the current status of women in America; information related to the global history and treatment of women; strategies for social evolution and the way forward. Basically, each chapter is only a snapshot to introduce you to the topics because so much information has the potential to be its own book. The High-Heel Footprint is aimed at the personal development of women, and the need for organizations to provide a better workplace for women. The years 2017 and 2018 have been declared the years of the woman! From here forward, we will continue this declaration! The evolution of the High-Heel Footprint and advancement of the female in society seems like a slow-motion movie to me. The struggles of women have been difficult over the centuries. Attention to the social needs of women seems to fizzle and then explode again. The cycle of wash, rinse, repeat, get dirty seems never-ending. If we look back on history, women have made great strides with the Women's Suffrage Movement from 1848 to 1920 (yes, it took that long to get the right to vote!). Despite this progress, several women continue to struggle for equal pay and higher-ranking career positions. We still experience discrimination,

misogyny, organizational barriers, and violence. Right now (again) in our world timeline, there is a rising female presence and voice. This is a call to be on that wave together and let the ripple continue to roll. Let it consume the status quo. Raise your voice, define your footprint and find your higher purpose!

Although the High-Heel Footprint Movement aims to strengthen the personal development of women and improve the way organizations provide equities for women, there have been recent political and controversial issues in the news, which have again raised awareness and controversy related to women's rights. In efforts to set the stage as to why we need to promote the High-Heel Footprint Movement, I would like to share some of these news highlights. On the political front, our 2016 presidential election had a female major-party candidate in the forefront. Her name was Senator Hillary Clinton. According to the national election polls, 43 percent of women voted for Clinton, but the women's vote was divided by race. The majority of non-college-educated white women (61%) voted for the male candidate, while 34 percent backed Clinton, and 5 percent voted otherwise. The majority of Clinton supporters were non-white women, Hispanic, or black. Donald Trump, the male candidate, won the election as the 45th

President of the United States with 304 electoral college votes to Clinton's 227 votes. The popular vote included 62,979,636 for Trump and 65,844,610 for Clinton. There is a debate that continues as to whether Trump won a fair race.

In January 2017, over 673 Women's Marches occurred worldwide that included over seven million women. The marchers protested and advocated for better legislative policies regarding human rights and other issues such as immigration reform, LGBTQ (Lesbian, Gay, Bi-sexual, Transgender, Questioning) rights, racial equality, health-care reform, and reproductive rights. Most of the rallies followed the inauguration of the 45th president of the United States and were sparked as a result of number 45's offensive statements against women. There is nothing honorable or amusing about racism or misogyny.

In reference to other 2017–2018 news headlines, women became silence breakers. On February 8, 2017, the Republican GOP (Grand Old Party – a nickname), verbally attempted to silence Senator Elizabeth Warren for criticizing the nomination of Jeff Sessions as unfit to serve as the United States attorney general. Senator Warren was reading a 30-year-old letter written in 1986 by Coretta Scott King, an American civil rights leader and widow of

Dr. Martin Luther King Jr. Ms. King's letter was written on letterhead from the Martin Luther King Jr. Center for Nonviolent Social Change Inc., and expressed sincere opposition to the confirmation of Jefferson B. Sessions as federal district court judge in the 1980s for the Southern District of Alabama. Ms. King's letter criticized him for using the powers of his office to deny access to black people to vote in the south. The GOP's aim to deny Senator Warren's right to read Ms. King's letter was followed by objections and disrespectful comments. The GOP tried to silence Senator Warren as she read Ms. King's letter. This is an example of courageous, smart women leaders expressing their voice. The message of their appeal was to stop the madness of voting for dishonorable people into office to lead our country.

Also in the news, the Me-Too Movement gave more women the courage to be silence breakers. Women who experienced sexual harassment or abuse, learned to stand up to their abusers, confront their sexual predators, and send them to prison. Hundreds of thousands of women who have experienced sexual assault from dominating men in their workplace or personal circles are standing together with the Me-Too Movement to support survivors. Founded in 2006 by Tarana Burke, the movement helps survivors of sexual violence find pathways to healing and empathy. The hashtag "Me Too" was inspired by the American actress and activist, Alyssa Milano, who's twitter message turned into global replies. Her tweet read "if you've been sexually harassed or assaulted write 'me too' as a reply to this tweet." Me-Too aims to uplift radical community healing as a social justice issue committed to disrupting all systems that allow sexual violence to flourish or be ignored. #MeToo

As a result of ongoing Hollywood sexual scandals of abuse and harassment gaining notoriety, even more women started speaking up. The Time's Up movement was formed in 2017 by Hollywood executives, actors, agents, writers, directors, and producers. The Time's Up movement combats workplace sexism through legal recourse, not just in the entertainment industry, but in industries across the country. The initiative creates legislation to penalize companies that tolerate harassment and discourage the use of nondisclosure agreements that have helped silence victims of abuse in the past. It includes a legal defense fund administered by the National Women's Law Center's Legal Network for Gender Equity connects victims of sexual harassment with legal representation. Time's Up established a GoFundMe account that raised millions of dollars. #TimesUp

Becoming "woke" is a slang term that has slightly evolved over time. In 2017, as a result of the Hollywood sex scandals, actresses began to relate this term to social injustice. They suggested that women find themselves a "woke man," meaning men who are aware of these female injustices and who are supportive. This assumes that men who are not woke, lack sensibilities, have sleeping minds, are immoral womanizers, and lack knowledge of the social issues and oppression faced by women. I could go on about this, but I think you understand my point. If a man is not standing up for a woman, and lifting her up, then he is wasting her time. There is no greater attribute than a strong man, who is loving, trustworthy, and encouraging. If you are a woman, tolerating an un-woke man, please wake yourself up.

On the economic front, the female consumer is responsible for 85 percent of household purchases, including vacations, family needs, and health care. Women are the primary income provider in 40 percent of households. With women working both outside of the home and in home-based businesses, marketers should pay close attention to the buying power of women.

In 2017, the U.S. Women's National Team in soccer finally won their victory for equal pay. There were also a record number of

Women CEO promotions in Fortune 500 companies. In 2018, the Notorious RBG's movie hit the theater depicting the life story of Honorable Ruth Bader Ginsburg - the second woman appointed to the US Supreme Court in the dominant culture of American men. She serves as an icon and trailblazer to fight for women's legal issues related to equality and choice. My favorite female wins, however, were for my heroine, Wonder Woman, and the director of her movie, Patty Jenkins. In June 2017, the blockbuster movie became the highest-grossing film ever by a female director. Congratulations on all of these wins for womankind!

Now what? Now that we have momentum again, how do we bring about social change that lasts? We start with the personal development of the individual woman who should be taking action and accountability for her own life. If you have the assistance of a woke man to help amplify you, that is wonderful, however, it is important to understand that nobody else is responsible for your choices or your happiness, but you. Next, we increase awareness and strategies for organizational accountability related to elevating women in the workplace. Finally, we decrease our tolerance for social inequities and poor leadership, while we pursue the need for social change. The High-Heel Footprint is just a new beginning. Let us find additional strategies together.

Chapter 1:
The High-Heel Footprint

The idea of developing both the personal and professional woman is a wholistic, as well as a holistic ideology. It is wholistic with the aim of developing the whole person and holistic at the same time, to inspire the mastery of your life, so you are in control of your mental, emotional and physical well-being. Although this book is aimed at women and organizations, if you are a man, reading this book, I applaud you for your openness, honor and courage. Women who are supported by good men are happier and have more success in their relationships and vice-versa. No matter if those relationships are friendships, colleagues or intimate.

> If you are a woman or a man reading this book, ask yourself how you are helping to amplify women either personally or professionally:
>
> _____
>
> I haven't thought about it _____

Many of the concepts and suggestions in this book are relative to both genders. Together, we are all part of the solutions for being better people. This book shares historical data reflecting the social challenges women have faced and continue to face. It provides strategies for personal and professional development. This is also a call to action, for organizations to evolve by eliminating the glass ceiling, which creates barriers toward the professional advancement of women.

Why are several women still struggling in the job market? Women are still underpaid, making only 80 cents to the dollar compared to men for the same work (2017, U.S. Department of Labor). This book identifies the challenges of women and provides strategies for them to elevate their life as they apply their strengths to serve their purpose. It is my hope that whether you are a woman or a man reading this book, that it helps you to find your talents and strengths to influence others, so you are inspired to become an agent of positive social change.

Why *The High-Heel Footprint*? Because most women love high-heels! The iconic actress Marilyn Monroe once said: "Give a girl the right shoes and she can conquer the world!" The High-Heel Footprint concept, which I created, uses the notion of the environmental footprint with a humorous twist. The High-Heel Footprint means relating your shoes to reflect your values, choices, and impact you make during your lifetime. This analogy is not only about heels. It's about wearing whatever shoes you feel comfortable in. Because everyone has the choice to step into whatever shoes they want to each and every day, then you also have the freedom to choose your attitude, emotions, and behaviors. Nobody else is responsible for your choices, except for you. **The High-Heel Footprint metaphor means you master your life to serve yourself and others.**

Although reducing and improving our environmental footprint means helping to save our planet—and there are many wonderful ways to do this—that is a story for a different book.

Your High-Heel Footprint is meant to be increased, improved, and value-added for yourself and others. Each person has a unique footprint. In what and where you choose to step is the key strategy to defining your purpose.

    We all have choices to wear different types of shoes. We also have free will, which allows us to make our own choices in life that either keep us on one path or redirects us toward another. Did you know that how we respond to our present is always in our control? This includes our thoughts, our feelings, and our behavior that leaves our footprint. What does your footprint toward humanity look like?

Are you helping to make the world a better place?
Yes ___ How? _____
No ___   I haven't thought about it ___

Are you helping to create positive social change?
Yes ___ How? _____
No ___   I haven't thought about it ___

Have you identified your talents, strengths, purpose?
Yes ___ What are they? _____
No ___   I haven't thought about it ___

How do the choices you make relate to your attitude and actions? Your footprint can be defined in many ways. Figuratively we know that not all heels are created equal. Some heels are high, others are low, and sometimes there are no heels at all. The High-Heel Footprint aims to enlighten you toward getting your heel unstuck and perhaps finding a new way of doing things that take you into a more comfortable stride of life. Make a difference in

humanity by sharing your strengths. Leave your High-Heel Footprint!

Can the very state of your current life situation directly reflect your footwear? Think about it: Footwear can be comfortable, irritating, stylish, sexy, sassy, sporty, safe, beachy, or weatherproof. There are also those bare-naked-feet people who don't like to wear shoes at all. The big question I have for you is, what type of footprint are you leaving as you walk this earth? Do your footprint or shoes make a statement? Do they add to the foundation of who you are? How do you use your stride to make an impact or footprint wherever you go? Do you walk in sync with others, or do you walk all over them? Do you tread lightly, or do you stomp? Do you wear sad, broken shoes and have regular pity parties for yourself? Where your feet take you can make a difference as to where you land, and what you do or do not accomplish in life . . . and yes, you may wear different types of shoes, depending on what you are doing. Stop and consider, which shoes are your favorite and why? How do you truly want to feel, and what shoes will take you there? Go High-Heel Footprint shopping now in your soul and find the most incredible shoes to wear that will leave your impactful footprint in the world. Let go of things that are not value-added to your life. Unstick your awful, pitiful heels . . . toss 'em away and master your life.

What if . . . choosing your emotions, attitude, and behavior every day were like choosing what shoes you will wear? What if stepping into your greatness took you to new levels of fulfillment? Anyone can achieve their own greatness or demise. Our choices, emotions, attitude, and behavior are a few things that are totally in our control, unless we have a chemical imbalance or need medical or mental help support. Nobody is ever too sovereign to seek help. If you are faced with a difficult life situation, please consider seeking the help of a physician or mental health professional. It can be the difference toward becoming a healthier you.

Sometimes we feel full of emotion because the path we are on is a bit rocky. Maybe you feel barefoot and alone in your struggle. In reference to this path, I'd like to share one of my favorite poems, written by Mary Stevenson (1936), called "Footprints in the Sand":

> One night I dreamed I was walking along the beach with the Lord. Many scenes from my life flashed across the sky. In each scene, I noticed footprints, other times there was only one.

This bothered me because I noticed that during the low periods of my life, when I was suffering from anguish, sorrow, or defeat, I could see only one set of footprints, so I said to the Lord,

"You promised me, Lord, that if I followed you, you would walk with me always. I have noticed that during the most trying periods of my life there has only been one set of footprints in the sand. Why, when I needed you most, have you not been there for me?"

The Lord replied, "The years when you have seen only one set of footprints, my child, is when I carried you."

Photo: Dr. Mo, Malibu California 2018
Marie Gregorio-Oviedo, Photographer

Find inspiration in your footprint to:

- Realize that you are not alone
- "**Walk**" toward value-added and empowering choices
- "**Step**" into the looking glass to face and eliminate any fears
- "**Hop**" toward personal goals to transform your life
- "**Dance**" in your magic shoes and find your "muchness," like Alice (in Wonderland) because you are worth it!

A Summary of How I Developed My High-Heel Footprint:

In my personal life, I have experienced numerous obstacles. Although they were challenging at the time, I eventually learned to shift my thinking to realize those obstacles were painful blessings that made me a better person. They developed my strength, character, and resilience. Resilience is "the strength and ability to overcome setbacks." Resilience means you identify and use coping skills, get back up after you have been down, and bounce back, rebound, adjust, adapt, rise above, rebuild, and learn to have grit and redirect yourself with a new plan and path.

I'm sharing my story with you not to compare or say that my tragedies are bigger than yours, because they may not be.

Everyone has their own story. My point is, whatever your story is, instead of complaining about it, find the good in your situation and create solutions and a vision for a new path. Let go of old baggage and pain. There is nothing more annoying than someone who consistently complains about others and their life. Please stop having your own pity party. Don't be that person. Move forward with positive solutions for a better life. Question any negative beliefs you may have at any time and release your suffering. Start telling people how you overcame your obstacles. Start changing the way you think and speak and begin creating a new life of resilience. If what you are doing now is not working in your favor, whether it be a job, relationship, health, living situation, etc., then start by doing something different to change your situation. Take charge and master your life. The first step toward finding your purpose and strengths is to shift your thoughts from negative to positive. The next step is to do just that – take one step to change something. Do something different even if it is a small change. Then take another step toward changing your situation. Find supportive people to help you. Several small steps will lead you to progress if you maintain a commitment toward yourself and keep the momentum going. If you do nothing, you get nowhere. Find solutions to keep moving you forward toward transformation and progress because you are worth it!

To help you understand the evolution of my high-heel footprint, I will begin with a summary of my childhood shoes, which are the foundation of who I am. I grew up in a very loving and stable middle-class American family. I am a sibling to three older brothers, an older sister and younger sister. Our parents were the best parents in the world. They provided us with a fair balance of discipline and freedom to become good people. I love my family very much. Although I was born in California, my ancestry shows that we are Iberian, from the Mediterranean. My descendants are from Spain, Italy, Portugal, Greece and the Canary Islands. My Spanish lineage is of royal blood from the Spanish Crowns of Aragon. My great, great Grandparents whom settled in the New Mexico territories in the 1600's were Conquistadors. This makes my family long-time settled Americans, prior to the Europeans who settled in the 1800's. Nonetheless, I want to remind everyone that the American Nation should always be a tribute to the original Native Americans, whose land we outsiders invaded. America was shaped by immigrants, but never forget that the Native-American's were here first.

I am blessed to say my childhood was nearly perfect. This created a strong foundation for the development of who I am as a person. I have grown up with little fear, lots of love and tons of confidence. I am tolerant of much and consider myself a fair person because of my self-esteem and personal life experiences. Although I question judgment and human inequities, I try to maintain an optimistic attitude about life. I was born in Southern California in December 1965 during a full moon. According to astrology, I am a Sagittarius with Leo rising. Both are fire signs. My Myers-Briggs evaluation shows that my personality is an ENTJ. Extrovert – energized by spending time with others; iNtuition – I focus on ideas and concepts with creativity and vision, while taking facts and details to a greater level; Thinking – prefer to be planned and organized; Judging – driven to lead others.

During the 1960's circa in America (era of my newness into the world), Lyndon B. Johnson was the 36th President of the United States; the Vietnam War was in full fight. The average annual wage was $7,000. The average cost of a "new" home was $13,000. The price of gasoline was .31 cents. The Civil Rights Movement led by Dr. Martin Luther King Junior and Cesar Chavez continued to march for Minority-American human rights. Hippies wore psychedelic clothing. Pop culture music included the Beatles, the Rolling Stones and Tom Jones, while Mary Poppins and the Sound of Music debuted at the box office.

My high school experiences in the early 1980s were a blast! I attended El Monte High School in California. My school offered a wonderful mix of academics, leadership, athletics and the arts. If you have ever seen the television show called "Glee" – this is what I compare my high school to when I attended. I received a well-rounded education. I had to change my shoes regularly as I was developing my footprint, because I was involved in several school and extracurricular activities. In addition to being an honor student, and in school government, the other shoes I wore will give you an idea of my activities. My footprints included Vans-skaters, dance slippers, choir heels, theatre shoes, songleading shoes, softball cleats, basketball shoes, track cleats, macramé loafers, and surf summer sandals.

Although this was a fun time in my life, it was also stressful because I had to learn to balance my personal life with academics and a lot of curricular activities. I was very involved, but I loved high school! After graduation, my young adult life consisted of wearing comfortable tennis shoes or sandals for walking around my university campus, professional heels for work, and then my sexy party heels for the very occasional night out. I was not a big partyer while attending Long Beach State University in California because I was extremely focused on academics. I initially took many science courses because my academic goal was to attend medical school to be a medical doctor. I was a science wiz, and especially excelled in biology. I ended up getting married to Angel, my high school sweetheart at age twenty-one while I was a junior in college, studying science. Although I told Angel that I was not interested in marriage because I planned to focus on my medical career, he would not take no for an answer. As a result of starting a family early in our twenties, I didn't think I could handle medical school (even though I was an honor student). I wish I had a mentor back then to give me better advice. My Mother and Aunts, who were queen of the Catholics also convinced me that I should marry Angel because he was such a great guy (he was!). As a result, I gave up my dream of being a physician and shifted my career plan to be a high school teacher and college professor. I taught both health and biology. This was one of those choices I lived to regret the rest of my life.

When I was twenty-four, my husband Angel committed suicide, and I was widowed with our two small children, Tahnie

and Joshua. Six months after my husband's death in 1990, my best girlfriend, Roseanne passed away from cancer. During this tragic time in my life, I had to think quickly on my feet. My shoes were a variety of pitiful-sad shoes, young widow-mommy shoes, snap-out-of-it comfortable shoes, innovative business shoes, and smart social-change shoes. Ten years after Angel's death, I remarried a handsome man named Steve in Ojai California. During our marriage I went back to school to graduate with a Master's in Public Health. My Master's Thesis was a Mental Health Curriculum. I utilized some of the mental health strategies as teaching lessons for my college students, myself, as well as counseled friends and family members. I became a regular counselor to everyone. Steve and I had a third child, named Bradley when I was age 30. Although Steve was a good father and there were happy times, our relationship ended up being tumultuous and we ended it with a bitter two-year divorce process. I was age thirty-seven at the time of our divorce and had just been diagnosed with breast cancer. I had quit teaching high school when I met Steve to establish a consulting business so I could work from home and balance my time as a mom and career woman. Even though Steve was not around to help me through my cancer ordeal and I was mostly alone, working from home helped me find time

to undergo chemotherapy and balance my life. Chemo was extremely hard on my body and it made me very ill for 6-days straight every time I had my infusion treatments. Fortunately, I had one of the top oncologists in the field. His name is Evan Slater. Yes, I lost my hair as well, but vanity left me, while my illness took over. It was a tough time in my life. I never told my oncologist that Steve was not around until a later time. I drove myself to chemo, then straight home to be ill. I was grateful for the main people who did help me through my painful chemo phase. This included my daughter Tahnie, who was still in high school, my two young son's Josh and Brad who did the best they could to give me love, my sister Suzette, my friend Suzanne Nunez Taylor who brought me flowers regularly, my mother-in-law Victoria Fields, my friends Sandy Casey, Shelly Burg, Rick Rust and the Oak View Little League parents who brought us food.

As a single mother with a home-based consulting business, I worried about my income a lot. Fortunately, due to my hard work and good character in the community, I never had to market my services. Word of mouth kept me busy with supportive clients. Early in my consulting business, I had an opportunity to work with high-level leaders who served the community. Writing is one of my strengths. Clients hired me to write community grant

proposals, conduct research, and offer program evaluation services. Securing large foundation and government funding for my clients helped provide an array of needed service initiatives to underserved communities. I helped my clients to help others while they served to create social change. I valued that, and it made me feel great about the work I did. I felt this was my purpose to "make a difference in humanity." The motto for my work became "when it's quality that counts." I wanted my clients to trust me with the quality work I provided them because my work benefited others like a ripple in a water droplet on the lake. Being an independent consultant provided a loving and balanced life for my children. It was a win-win situation.

  While I was undergoing my cancer treatments and surgeries, one of my client's – the Ventura County Public Health Department, offered me a job as an Administrator to oversee a three-county, regional social-change initiative called the Network for a Healthy California. This initiative served millions of people in California and I oversaw the Gold Coast region of San Luis Obispo, Santa Barbara and Ventura Counties. The program provided public health outreach and education related to nutrition, physical activity, walkable communities and local policy change. I chaired several collaborative committees including a 60-member committee in three counties consisting of staff from hospitals, clinics, schools, non-profits and government agencies. I enjoy working with diverse people. I also had a wonderful outreach and education staff. This was a good job, but the pay was low considering the responsibilities. As a result of my low income, I decided to apply to graduate school again and start teaching health 101 at Oxnard College. I already had a Master of Public Health degree and I thought a Doctorate would launch my career to a better level. All this while still enduring my cancer treatments and divorce. Yes, it was a crazy, challenging time in my life.

While I was in my thirties and forties, I began to experience one tragedy after another. There was a lot of death as my aunts and uncles and friends in my close circle departed. The more I experienced death, the easier it was to handle emotionally, and I became stronger. Because of my own grief, I learned how to counsel others with their grief. These major traumas had caused me to have a bit of post-traumatic stress disorder, but my ego never let me show it to my family or friends. In fact, not many people helped me because they thought "I was a strong woman." I mostly kept my sorrow to myself. I sought professional counseling, and I had a few friends to speak with, who I could count on. Unfortunately, time is slow, so healing of my soul was slow. This is when I could no longer see my footprints and I believe God started to carry me.

In the midst of my traumas, my career path had been severely altered. Even as an educated woman with strategic planning and teaching experience, I found jobs where I was underpaid to work on high-level projects. I have worked in male-dominated career fields, such as a county fire department and for the Department of Defense. As a result of low-paying jobs, I have had to move around my community frequently because I could not afford my rent. I sent out hundreds of resumes in search of higher paying jobs, but got nowhere. When I was age 45, I was in a major ski accident. I broke my tibia and fibula in seven places. I was bedridden for three months, with nearly a year of rehabilitation for my leg. I thought I would never walk again. My orthopedic surgeon, Dr. Emily Bensen was the best! She encouraged me, while she healed me. I also had the best physical therapists at the Ventura County Medical Center who never gave up on me during my painful recovery. I kept on telling people; not walking again was not an option. I had to undergo serious surgeries and worked hard to rebuild my strength. Each of these situations I have experienced in my adult life exhausted me. My shoes (AKA, footprints) were extremely weary and torn. What did I do? I idled

through my situations until I learned to change the way I thought about my predicaments and lifted myself up. I never felt sorry for myself. I always strived to get back up. I learned to love self-help books. I maintained an incredible amount of faith because I love God with all my heart and soul. I continued to pray and discovered meditation to find more peace. I have regularly re-identified my strengths and footprints. I stopped waiting for closed doors to open that were not serving me and found new paths. It was never easy, but because of my strong faith in God and willpower to change my life, I have always been able to find new direction. I refuse to allow anyone or anything to define who I am. My wise Mother Ida always told me "he/she who angers you, conquers you." I never forgot that. I learned to master my mind and my life to evolve my soul. I learned not to let little annoying things or people bother me. I learned to become a better and stronger person. Now I hope to help others by sharing my story and my knowledge in whatever forums or opportunities God presents me with. I work for him through my purpose.

Romans 12:2 in the Christian Bible says, "Don't be conformed to this world, but be transformed at the way we look at things, by the renewing of your mind." (New International Version 2011)

The Dalai Lama said, "We can never obtain peace in the outer world until we make peace with ourselves."

Life is a process. Although you may think you have not arrived at where you would like to be in life, I am here to tell you that you are on your way up whatever path you choose. Learn to master your mind. Learn how to remove obstacles that get in the way of your progress. Find a new path if the one you are on is not supporting you. Learn how to love yourself and eliminate your fears. FEAR can be thought of as Fantasized Experiences Appearing Real. Stop and become aware of the good things in your life. Be grateful. Enjoy them. Be patient and keep making progress. Keep on looking for the light in all things. I encourage you to look for and see the love of everything around you (family, friends, the good things in your life) and give thanks instead of focusing on the bad. Try not to compare yourself to others, because you are a unique and special person. God loves all people. Once you find your purpose, you will recognize your beauty. You will find peace. I believe in God. God and my spirit guides or guardian angels have helped me through everything. It took me a while to trust them, but now I am certain they are with me every day. We have our own personal relationship.

When I was in my early thirties and forties, I read a thought-provoking book that changed my life. It is called *Many Lives, Many Masters*, by Dr. Brian Weiss. Dr. Weiss is a psychotherapist and his book changed the way I thought about life and death. I grew up in the Catholic religion. I never learned about reincarnation. Dr. Weiss' book reveals how he learned to integrate past-life therapy to heal people's fears and anxieties. Dr. Weiss was an atheist turned Christian as a result of his discoveries, and now makes past-life regression therapy his life work. The message in Many Lives, Many Masters makes perfect sense to me. Our souls are re-born to learn lessons in life. If we do not learn them, we must return to the classroom of life. The lessons we may need to overcome can include greed, jealousy, anger, insecurities, fears, etc. My new spiritual awakening has strengthened my beliefs in God and the holy spirits that help and surround us. I believe that God loves everyone, no matter how bad you think you are. God wants us to be better people, so we must learn our lessons in order for our soul to evolve. I am now more aware of my purpose, mission and the direction of my life. Teaching the lessons I created from the High-Heel Footprint are part of my life mission.

Keys to Master Your Mind to Make a Difference:
- The reality that time heals. Try your best to be patient in all situations. Unfortunately, time can be slow, therefore causing frustration. Figure out what works to distract you and calm you down when you start feeling frustration (i.e., meditation, exercise)
- Engage in reciprocity from family and friends. Ask for help when you need it. Give permission to others to assist and support you.
- Maintain social connections and networking. Laugh and enjoy life. Isolation is not good for you.
- Therapy, life coaching, and confiding in a mentor, family or friend is very helpful.
- Please seek professional assistance from a physician if you are battling depression, hormonal imbalance, or other physical, mental, or emotional issues.
- Maintain physical activity and healthy eating habits.
- Live a healthy lifestyle. Find support to discontinue poisonous elements in your life, including substance abuse, alcohol, smoking, or toxic relationships.
- Practice creating boundaries for yourself, so you are prepared when people cross them.

- Work on strengthening your boundaries. Let go of issues or people that are not positive forces in your life. Find a different path to focus on that will add value to your life and put an end to your suffering.
- Do not compare yourself to others or beat yourself up. You are special. Love yourself.
- Believe in something (faith-based, spiritual, or other inspirational practices).
- Practice mindfulness, prayer, or meditation daily. Find your quiet peacetime.
- Practice gratitude daily. Choose to be happy!
- Look for and identify your sense of purpose/worthiness. What are your talents and strengths? What do you love to do? What makes you happy? Find your passion and do it. Create a plan to develop your strengths. Find resources to help you.
- Have a good attitude and maintain positive mental health. Seek help if you need it. Help yourself become strong before you help others.
- Set a goal.
- Identify the obstacles in your way.
- Identify strategies to overcome those obstacles.

- Identify strategies to keep you on the path to making a difference.
- If you choose to do nothing, nothing will change.

Chapter 2:
It's a Problem

Women remain underrepresented in the US and global workforce. According to the U.S. Department of Labor, their participation rate is predicted to rise at all levels in the twenty-first century. While societal factors, including education and cultural traditions, can compromise the career objectives of high-achieving women, the lack of major ongoing platforms further adds to the barriers of bringing these issues to the forefront. This book proposes to contribute to this edge of knowledge by identifying and analyzing relevant factors that challenge women. There are voices of women who continue to seek gender equality or professional advancement in the workplace, with more strategies needed to support female professionals. Unfortunately, some women continue to experience a dead-end career or the glass ceiling, no matter how qualified they are. I have personally experienced these types of inequities – despite having a doctoral degree. I have created amazingly successful programs for my

previous employers who have disappointed me with their lack of credibility, leadership and lack of amplification of women. There is a lot of talk and more action required to implement effective strategies for the personal and professional development of women. When I worked for the Department of Defense for example, I received an all-hands email from the technical director bragging about the six percent of women in the organization who made high-grade GS 13 and 14 salaries. As the Diversity Chair for Federally Employed Women at the time, I could not help myself from responding to him to let him know this statistic did not represent a good news story, considering the demographics. Changes need to be made to advance more women into high-level management positions.

Tables 1, 2 and Figure 1 show how women have flourished in the labor force between 2005 and 2015, and how they have excelled in the attainment of college degrees compared to men. As of 2018, however, women continue to make lower salaries than men for the same work.

Table 1
U.S. Women's Participation Rates, 2005 compared to 2015

(Hispanics, Blacks/African-Americans, Caucasians, Asians/Pacific Islanders, All Women)

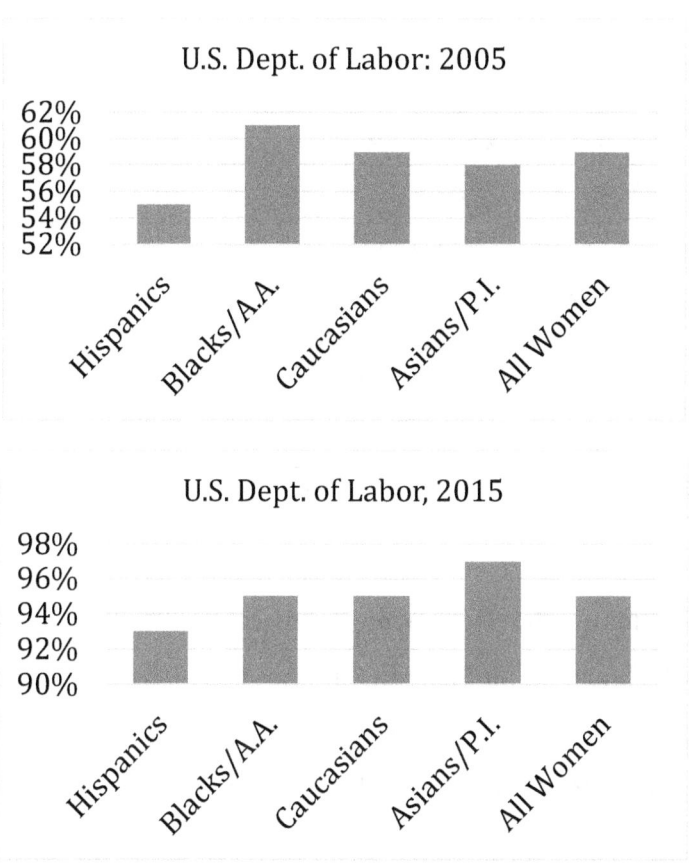

Median Weekly Earnings/Gender Wage Gap

(U.S. Department of Labor, Institute for Women's Policy Research, 1965–2016)
* Varies by occupation

Figure 1
Women's Earnings Compared to Men from 1965 to 2016

Year	Women's Percent Earnings vs. Men
1965	59.9%
1975	58.8% (+1.1%)
1985	64.6% (+5.8%)
1995	71.4% (+6.8%
2005	81.0% (+9.6%) Women $585/wk, Men $722/wk
2016	81.8% (+.8% or 21.9% less) Women $745/wk, Men $911/wk

Figure 1 shows women's earnings compared to men's, on average, from 1965 to 2016. In this fifty-three-year span, women only earned an average 21 percent increase in salary compared to men. This does not account for the low-wage earners who could not afford modern inflation.

Table 2
U.S. College Degrees by Gender and Culture

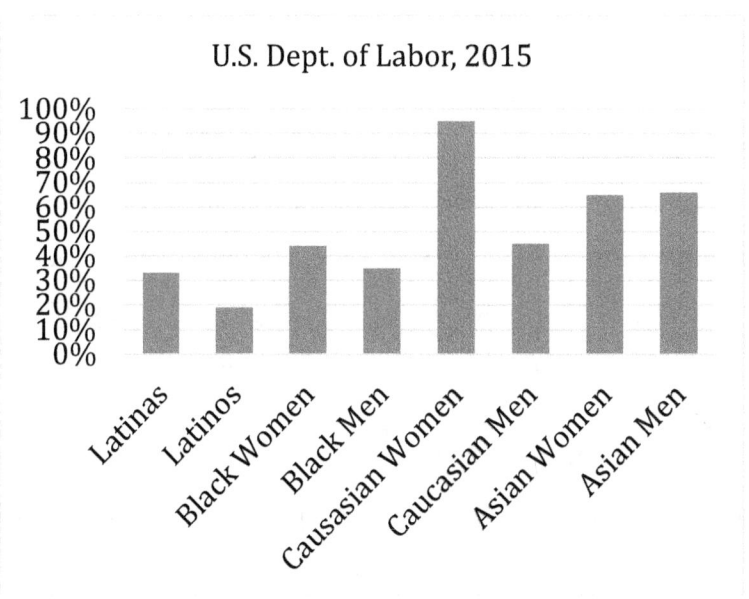

Table 2 shows the percent of college degrees attained by men and women from different American cultures in 2015. Historically, women have had low expectations to obtain an education/career, but have now exceeded college degrees compared to men. With more women in the workforce or starting their own business, they are educating themselves toward improved success related to their careers.

Although women have more management opportunities today, they still remain at a distance from powerful corporate positions. This factor, called "the glass ceiling," is an analogy of an invisible barrier keeping women, and especially minority women, from reaching top positions. Women who experience both gender and cultural biases experience double the frustration and discouragement, as they can see through the glass ceiling but cannot move on to achieve their goals. As a result, many of them accept career compromises because they simply need to survive.

Women of the twenty-first century have had opportunities to enter occupations previously closed to them. Women CEOs in Fortune 500 companies, female corporate officers, and women who serve on company boards, however, still remain few in number. Additionally, the volume of research consistently shows that black and Hispanic women remain at the bottom of the labor market by earning the lowest wages (U.S. Department of Labor, 2016). The most common discrimination charges reported by the Equal Employment Commission (2016) include women of color confronting both issues of race and gender. Caucasian women report that they rarely think in terms of race as opposed to gender in the workplace. According to the U.S. Department of Labor (2016), some Caucasian women do not understand issues of race in the workplace, because they have not experienced racial discrimination. While conducting my national research in 2008, women of color disclosed that issues related to race and ethnicity significantly influenced and challenged their work and personal lives. We owe much gratitude to the female trailblazers who moved the path of history in a better direction. For example, Victoria Chaflin Woodhull was the first woman nominated for president in 1872 when women were not even allowed to vote. Eleanor Roosevelt established the Commission on the Status of Women in 1961, which is dedicated to the promotion of gender equality and female empowerment. The Honorable Supreme Court Justice, Ruth Bader Ginsburg championed legal wins such as co-founding the ACLU (American Civil Liberties Union), civil rights, equal protection, the gender wage gap/pay discrimination, rights for those with disabilities and mental illness, LGBTQ rights, and a woman's right to choose. I highly recommend you see the movie "RBG" about the life of the Honorable Supreme Court Justice Ruth Bader Ginsburg. Malala Yousafzai is the youngest Nobel Prize winner for her work toward amplifying the global rights of women and girls. The upcoming section in this book called "the influence of feminism" will discuss more about female trailblazers and the history of how women have been marginalized globally.

The stress associated with independence, professional expectations, and balancing family and home comes at high psychological and social costs for all women. My research shows there is a difference, however, experienced by women of different cultures in comparison to other women. During the transition from traditional roles (working inside the home) to a professional role (working outside the home), the experiences by women of different cultures include the stress and psychological conflict of a threatened allegiance to their culture. This often leads to the abandonment of their ethnic identity, which creates guilt—another finding I established in my research.

My research also found that societal factors, including education, cultural practices, and traditions can influence or even compromise the career objectives of high-achieving women. Historical evidence, based on feministic theories has made a huge impact on the lives of women. Although the complexities and teachings of the past do not necessarily hold fast to all norms of the present, they have nonetheless contributed to society as we know it today.

As women of all ethnicities continue to contribute to the workforce as part of a global economy, they are slowly breaking

out of their traditional roles, transitioning from housewives and low-profile jobs to being better educated and entering new sectors of the job market. A good number of women are starting home-based businesses or other types of businesses because they are tired of waiting for a company to hire them or give them the pay raise they deserve.

Feministic theories share a belief that all women experience similar individual and social challenges. While women recognize the traditions associated with their subordination, they continue to experience areas of concern in the labor market and question what to do about it. The sandwich generations, for example, include people (both men and women) who are raising children, while also taking care of their parents or other elders. They are experiencing the need to find support and balance to their lives. Few companies offer childcare or family time off, which increases the stress of being the family caretaker, while also holding down a full-time job. While employers struggle to maintain their policies, it is also important to understand the challenges of its workforce and find solutions to supporting them.

The Influence of Feminism

Women have historically been raised with the belief that caring for and assisting others is of central importance to their life's work; many also believe their own strength develops as a result of this experience. As a woman develops her inner voice of knowing herself and valuing a quality life, a developmental transformation occurs in her relationships, self-esteem, morality, and behavior.

The principles of Feminism recognize the socialized differences between men and women, which have historically contributed to the oppression of women. Feminism is not a bad word, and it does not mean women dislike men. Women value and need men who are kind, respectful and supportive. Feminism does, however, recognize and stand up for the rights of women who have been marginalized and treated unfairly because of their gender, race, culture, sexual preference, age, diverse abilities, or religious affiliation. The rights of women have been influenced by both men and women. The Women's Rights Movement fought for women's suffrage in the United States from 1848 to 1920 but began as early as 1769 when US colonies adopted the English system of property ownership. Women could not own property or keep the earnings from the property. The history of organized feminism began in 1848 with the first women's rights convention in Seneca Falls, New York. The convention called for equal treatment of women and men under the law and voting rights for women. It was organized by Elizabeth Cady Stanton, a mother of four from upstate New York and Lucretia Mott, a Quaker abolitionist. The goals of women's suffrage were to address social and institutional barriers that limited women's rights, including family responsibilities, a lack of educational and economic opportunities, and the absence of a voice in political debates. Susan B. Anthony, who was a teacher in Massachusetts, was a key leader of women's suffrage in the 1850s. She created the National Women Suffrage Association (NWSA) to reform federal law of the Fifteenth Amendment, which excluded women from voting.

A summary of the Annenberg classroom files (annenbergclassroom.org) presenting a timeline of the US Women's Rights Movement from 1769 to 2009 is found on the following page.

Year	Event
1769:	Women request property rights
1848:	First Women's Rights Convention held
1868:	National Labor Union backs equal pay for equal work
1869:	Racial equality issue splits two suffrage associations
1869:	Territory of Wyoming gives Women right to vote
1872:	Congress requires federal equal pay for equal work
1872:	First woman nominated for president, Victoria Chaflin Woodhull. (Women were not yet allowed to vote)
1872:	Susan B. Anthony arrested for attempting to vote
1874:	Supreme Court denies the voting right to women
1896:	National Association of Colored Women organized
1903:	Women's Trade Union League established
1920:	The Nineteenth Amendment is ratified, giving women the right to vote
1920:	League of Women Voters established
1923:	First Equal Rights Amendment (ERA) introduced, stating that men and women shall have equal rights
1961:	Eleanor Roosevelt leads Commission on the Status of Women
1962:	Equal Pay Act becomes federal law
1964:	Title VII of the Civil Rights Act of 1964 is passed, barring employment discrimination based on race, sex, and other grounds
1965:	Supreme Court issues landmark ruling on legalizing the availability of contraceptives for American women
1967:	Civil rights protections extended to women (not just minorities)
1972:	Congress passes Title IX of the Education Amendment requiring schools to use federal funds equally for women and men
1973:	Supreme Court establishes abortion right in Roe v. Wade, giving a woman the right to choose (nullifying anti-abortion laws)
1973:	Eliminated women-only branches in US military
1978:	Banned employment discrimination against pregnant women
2009:	Lilly Ledbetter Fair Pay Act signed into law (giving workers the right to sue for pay discrimination)

There has been much work done related to the Women's Rights Movement, in addition to research and theories that have been unsung. The work of Carol Gilligan, for example, began in the 1970s during the resurgence of the Women's Rights Movement. Gilligan's research presents how women's voices have historically been left out in society. Gilligan's theory promoting "voice" sends a powerful message to humanity. Remember the story I referenced in the beginning of this book about how the republican GOP attempted to silence Senator Elizabeth Warren? Having a voice means being able to state your opinion. Having a voice also means having the right to make a decision related to something. It means being able to speak your truth and feel safe about it. The historical perpetuation of patriarchy is another example of research related to a key source of oppression for women. Case studies related to Patriarchy's influence on women are well documented in the Women's studies research of Garcia (1997), Isasi-Diaz (1988), Sharma (1987) and Villanueva (2002). Garcia's research, for example described traditional Latin culture as male-oriented and dominating. Similar case studies have further led to the oppression of women.

During the racial and social protests of the 1960s and 1970s in America, women of color, including African Americans and

Latinas, protested with community mobilization strategies, boycotts, marches, and demonstrations. Although Latina women shared multiple sources of oppression experienced by other women of color in history, such as African American, Asian American, and Native American women, internally, Latina women's struggles also dealt with fighting a male-dominated culture. When the social-civil rights of the feminist agenda raised voices of protests to challenge sexism and machismo, some men took notice, and some did not. At this time, traditional female roles became questioned, as did the patriarchal constraints, further adding to Latina tensions and oppression. Modern-day Latina development combines freedom from cultural bondage, empowerment, and new social opportunities as an expression of the liberation toward self.

When I was awarded my doctoral degree in 2009, only five-percent of Hispanic women had graduated in America with doctoral degrees (4,109 Latinas out of a total of 78,890 doctoral degrees were conferred by postsecondary institutions). From 2014 to 2015, US Latina doctoral degrees rose to seven percent and included 6,246 out of 93,626 (National Center for Educational Statistics, retrieved from nces.ed.gov, 2018). This remains an alarming statistic and reminds me of how hard I have worked. People who cannot appreciate that, do not understand the dedication and strive for life balance that goes into attending graduate school. To add to my challenge, I completed my courses, colloquial and dissertation research during cancer diagnosis and treatment, divorce, and raising my three young children. It took seven years, but I did it! I earned a Ph.D. is in Education and Knowledge Management. God truly carried me through this challenging part of my life. So, when I meet people who treat me unfairly or are confrontational due to their insecurities within themselves, I remind myself of my strengths, character, and good will toward humanity to achieve my purpose. It keeps me in check. If, however, I feel the need to express my voice, or stand up for the underserved, I do. My two biggest pet peeves are men that do not actively support or recognize the hard work of women, and the second is women who find a way to stomp on or over the women they fear or are intimidated by. My suggestion to them is to stop and take an honest look at examining your own footprint. We must to be lifting each other up!

Modern-day women must strategize to balance their worlds with respect to achieving professional success and leadership status. Today there are several global movements led by women to support the rights of the unheard, underpowered, and underserved. Global movements for peace, equality, advancement, protection, empowerment, and solidarity continue to break down walls of obstruction and build bridges toward freedom. The fearless voices calling for the freedom and advancement of humanity must never be silenced. We must continue to move forward with more determination because a move backward is unacceptable.

The Influence of Culture, Religion and Spirituality

This section is not based on my opinion and it is not meant to offend any religion or culture. As stated before, I believe in God, and I believe with all of my heart that God loves all people, however, based on research, there have been men who have influenced the degradation of women throughout history. Although there is much more to say about several historical examples that have influenced the personal and social development of women, this section only highlights a few to give you an idea of how the issue with misogyny and the marginalization of women has perpetuated since the beginning of time. Some cultures have shifted from their ancient practices to become more respectable to women and some have much more to do to advance the freedoms of women. Between the 1800s and 1900s, as the population of the US multiplied sevenfold, women began to enter the labor market. "Nearly all of these were poor women whose work both at home and in the labor market was essential to the survival of the working-class family" (Ruether, 1981, p. 176). As a result, places of worship noted their concern regarding women in the public workforce as interfering with their divinity and roles in the home as mothers, homemakers, nurses, and educators (p. 177). According to Ruether, (1981), the boundaries between the secular and feminists in America during the twentieth century began to shift toward women questioning their expectations by places of worship and their roles in society. Historical American culture and religion has strongly influenced gender inequality, reproductive rights, economic rights, and social inequality as a result of patriarchal dominance. Although this historical context can be linked to the psychological and social development of women, personal choice, and patterns of social change, modern-day issues are related to the need for continued social change, autonomy and opportunity. It is my right (as is yours) to respect only good leaders who are capable of creating change with the characteristics of honor, integrity and humility. Mutual respect for the greater good of the world, society, and organizations is required for social change, otherwise the noise of distraction is interfering with the flow of good energy and human progress.

> My Achilles heel is the incompetence and/or ignorance of people in leadership roles who are not trustworthy or who lack character and respect for the people they serve. What you do when I am not looking – matters!

For centuries, various cultures and tribes around the world have influenced the status of women in society. Cultural laws, religion or spiritual practices have influenced the norms of how women were defined and treated. The dominated patriarchal societies have mostly been responsible for creating their own laws, rules or norms, due to their fear of female power. In addition to Judaism and Christianity, other global spirituality practices have influenced the social development of women. Buddhism, Hinduism, Confucianism, Taoism, American, Greek, Latin, African, Chinese, Egyptian and Syrian cultures, for example, have had strong influences on the ideologies imposed on women (Foreman, 2016). Although there are many cultures which have maintained patriarchal dominations, there are a few matriarchal cultures that continue to thrive.

A matriarchy is a society where females have a central role in politics, leadership, moral authority, and control of property. Female led societies have included the Minangkabau of West Sumatra, Indonesia, for example. The Minangkabau are considered one of the largest matriarchal societies known today. They believe the mother is the most important person in society requiring property to be bequeathed from mother to daughter as tribal law. While the clan chief is usually male, women select the chief and can remove him from office, should they feel he failed to fulfill his duties. The Mosuo's of Yunnan and Sichuan provinces are other matriarchal societies who live near the border of Tibet. The Mosuo live in large households with property passed down from the matriarch. Mosuo women handle business decisions. Children take the mother's name. Women choose their partners. African and Egyptian tribes have elevated women with matriarchal queens such as Queen Candace Amanirena of Nubia, Queen Nefertiti of Egypt, and Queen Makadea of Ethiopia. Tribes with female rulers have promoted considerable autonomy over the lives of women. There have been women in global history who have blazed a trail to change the status and roles of women, and there have also been male leaders who sought power by excluding women from political and social positions of status. Unfortunately, there have

also been male leaders throughout history who have omitted facts in historical writings relative to some female leaders in efforts to diminish their successes (Moloi, 2013).

Historical American, Latin, Greek, and Syrian history, for example, shows how men of power barred women from public status by keeping them in the home. According to Dr. Amanda Foreman (2017), ancient Greek culture vied to maintain male honor and control. For example, in efforts to depict the strength and power of masculinity, male Greek leaders authored stories about the slaying of mythological Amazon women by centaurs in pictorials and community statues. Greek women were not allowed to vote, were forced to wear veils and had no equal rights to men. The Greek philosopher Aristotle said, "Women were not as perfect as men and were incapable of reason, therefore, must be controlled by men." Greek mythology also created the ideology of Pandora's Box. Pandora was like Eve, the first female on Earth. Pandora is armed with a jar or box (similar to the concept of a woman's womb). If the womb or box gets opened (via intercourse), she will release evils into the world. As a result, woman need to be bound and a veil is a symbol to cover her or bind her. Syrian cultural laws had also reduced the status of women as a result of militaristic conquest, control and patriarchal domination. Men could do

anything, but women would suffer for their own transgressions or any wrong-doing of the men in their lives (husbands or male relatives). Women must not remove their veils in public and be covered or they were punished or killed (Foreman, 2016)

    Confucianism originated in China in the 5th century BC by Confucius. Confucian-influence extends to Korea, Japan and Vietnam. Confucianism is a patriarchal religious way of governing. Confucianism is similar to the Latin ideologies of male machismo. It created a social order where women remain at the bottom. Women are to remain inside the home. The philosophy of the Dao or Taoism requires the obedience of women to their fathers, husbands and eldest sons. The concepts of the yin and the yang are symbols related to Chinese philosophy to create the balance of energy in the world. The yin and yang represent opposing forces such as downward vs. upward, darkness vs. light. The yin represents the soft female essence and the yang is the powerful male essence. The yin and yang concept were created by male leaders because women were seen as a threat to their power. Similar to the teachings of the various Christian religious secs, religious documents written by dominant men declared that "God said" this is what is to be, therefore, people believed the ideology of women's' inferiority must not be challenged out of fear of what

God might do to them (Foreman, 2016). Interpretation, power and control are responsible for the creation of belief systems and social norms of behavior. As a modern woman, who has experienced much, I find it hard to believe that my God who loves all people, would subject women to such harsh, non-value added and dishonorable treatment.

During the Babylonian Empire, certain laws protected women, but forbid economic or sexual freedom. This further legitimized patriarchy by designating the virginity of a woman as a condition for marriage. As a result, the father of the woman would suffer a lower price over his daughter's dowry if she was not a virgin. The daughter would also not be able to own land, but could control it upon her husband's death to determine what child would receive the inheritance. If a woman was not obedient to her husband, she would be punished or killed. Throughout the history of patriarchal societies, men have wiped out the stories and names of powerful women in the history books to distract the truth about those women who had prominently influenced their cultures (Foreman, 2016).

Buddhism is an ancient practice founded by Buddha Shakyamuni, a royal prince born in 624 BC in the India/Nepal region. His discovery of meditation and enlightenment teaches people about liberating their suffering. Buddhism's universal message is that gender is meaningless. This offered women the opportunity to shatter the concept of the yin and yang and gave women preferential treatment.

Wu Zetian was the only female emperor in Chinese history to rule during the Tang Dynasty between 618 – 907 CE. At this time, Tang women were unveiled and possessed freedom of thought and equality. During the Tang Dynasty, both women and men achieved opportunities through merit. The fall of Emperor Wu's historical leadership was a result of men who made up horrible stories about her, to try to illegitimize her greatness.

During the era of hunters and gatherers, Nomadic Eurasian tribes valued the social roles of women as greater than those roles of men. Women were highly valued for their talents and contributions to society. For example, women who learned about the medicinal powers of plants became powerful and respected healers. Women's skills also included making leather, tools and were great tattoo artists. Nomadic women contributed to the military success of their tribes. They were strong warriors who were also valued for their sniper skills using bows and arrows. In

400 BC in Mongolia, China, India and Persia, the Khan princess, who was the daughter of Genghis Khan, was a powerful leader. She became the Ice Maiden of Altai. Genghis Khan led women warriors and provided women with powerful opportunities (Foreman, 2016).

    The ancient spirituality of meditation was commonly practiced in the fifth and sixth century BC by Eastern cultures. Modern-day spirituality practices have shifted to include prayer and/or meditation. Modern Americans use meditation, simple breathing and relaxation exercises to unplug from stress and find a state of peace, mindfulness for self-observation, awareness, and transformation. The term meditation itself has an evolved meaning for different people. The benefits of meditation, relaxation, or breathing exercises are said to relate to improved mental and physical well-being. It can be a time to find quiet, relax and recharge your mind and body. Today not all people who meditate are necessarily spiritual or of an Eastern religion. Many people still believe in God, Christianity, or a universal creator and continue to pray. The modern-day transition for those who have felt restricted by the boundaries of their culture or religion have left places of worship to pray in their own silence and find their personal relationship with God. Meditation has been added to their lives as a support system for holistic healing.

There are many religions that continue to encourage hope and faith and teach people to care for themselves and others with a dedication to God. Spiritual practices and attending or not attending a place of worship is a personal choice. Serving your community and family in the manner you choose to is also a personal choice. I have much respect for the amazing wives, husbands, mothers and fathers who make the world and their family-life thrive as a result of love.

Diversity and Inclusion in the Workplace

General diversity in the workforce is important for today's global economy. General diversity means people have different educational backgrounds, skills and talents. Diversity and inclusion of gender in the workplace should provide females with the opportunities for advancement without barriers. This means offering training opportunities or recognizing qualified and educated women for the same jobs as men in the field. The glass ceiling continues to exist and remains an analogy that represents a barrier faced by women in the workplace. Female diversity and inclusion efforts must continue to break the glass ceiling for those

who are educated or qualified to attain high-level career positions. As a result of that ceiling, women are separated from important management positions and are also not equally represented in comparison to men in the workforce. Male-dominated organizations have historically deprived women of certain rights. As a result, women have experienced inequities in both career and personal life. Inequities in career include compensation, promotion, and advancement to middle- and high-level positions. Inequities in personal life include trying to balance family life with flex time, job-sharing, and support. Women also need to realize their role in their advancement. Take responsibility for your education, sign up for trainings, sit at the table and offer your knowledge at company planning meetings. Volunteer for special projects to get more experience. Find a mentor to guide you. Amplify the ideas of other women at the table who are often ignored.

As office machines developed during the late nineteenth century and early twentieth century, the work for women shifted to telephone operators and clerical work, such as bookkeeping, stenography, and typing, to keep up with office jobs. As these positions became dull, routine jobs, male clerks who occupied these positions went on to college and sought management positions, leaving the less desirable jobs for the women. Women also remained strong in human service positions such as nurses, librarians, social workers. The Equal Pay Act of 1963, Title VII of the 1964 Civil Rights Act, affirmative action, and the formation of the Equal Employment Opportunity Commission helped women move up in the labor market between 1970 and 1990 to secure management and professional positions. To avoid challenges with climbing the corporate ladder, women entrepreneurs are establishing their own businesses to create their own work schedule in an effort to find a balance between work and family. They're also doing it because some women in corporate positions have become uncomfortable with the decreased quality of life experienced as a result of a hectic work schedule.

Diversity and inclusion should not create additional burdens on companies. Diversity and inclusion should not be an obligation, but an opportunity to make a difference for employers to expand their ways of thinking, doing business, and maintaining global competitiveness. A diverse workforce allows people to network and build on their differences and teamwork to find harmony as an organizational culture. Recommendations to organizations for success include:

- Recruit a diverse workforce through affirmative action resources to increase representation of women and minorities;
- Form employee resource groups to include a team for women's leadership and other diversity teams that foster an environment of respect and inclusion;
- Survey employees regarding diversity and inclusion issues; then finding solutions together
- Collaborate on strategies to eliminate both intentional and unintentional bias
- Provide progress reports at meetings; to create sustainability
- Make leadership accountable for hiring a diverse workforce and require them to oversee the development, retention, and promotion of their employees.

Chapter 3: Strategies for the Personal Evolution of Your Footprint

Define Your Footprint Based on Your Day/Situation:

Slippers: Relaxing, Content, Stress-free

Sandals: Fun, Fresh, Friendly

Flats: Soft, Treads Lightly, Canny, Genuine, Caring, Comforting

Low Heel: Mature, Wise, Empathetic, Enlightened, Contributor, Somewhat Safe

Medium Heel: Busy, Smart, Strategist, Leader, Confident, Collaborator

High Heel: Courageous, Independent, Sexy, Daring, Competitive

Boots: Hard-working, Self-sufficient, Wanderer, Free Thinker, Protective, Very Safe

Athletic Shoes: Strong, Sturdy, Energetic, Team Player, Active, Competitive, Brawny, Powerful

Barefoot/Shoeless: Environmentally Conscientious, Free, Comforting, Exposed, Natural

Healthy Choices Will Add Value to Your Life

The Topic of Choices:

- Some choices are value-added or honorable
- Some choices are non-value-added or dishonorable
- The ability to control your choices takes practice and repetition—it's like exercising your brain

This may sound obvious, and I will say it again throughout this book: We always have the choice to be in control of our emotions and other decisions we make. If you are experiencing sadness, depression, a chemical imbalance, or other disorder, please seek professional care because this will help you better control your emotions. If you are normally a healthy person of sound mind, then strive to master your mind. Often when life's expectations are not going our way, we begin to feel sad and think that our life is out of our control. When we experience disagreements within our relationships, our emotions and attitude can reflect pessimism, anger, or unhappiness. Sometimes those feelings are so strong they can consume us. They can fester inside our soul, like a sore that aches. In efforts to find our peace, we must "practice" making the choice to let go of negative feelings and frustrations. Fear is an example of a negative feeling. If you live in fear often, you live in worry. If you live in fear for your safety, you should learn to become more aware of your surroundings. Decrease your fear by becoming more vigilant. If you fear for your safety due to a physically or mentally abusive person in your life, then make the choice to let go of that person and seek professional help or legal protection. We sabotage ourselves if we live in generic fear of evolving our patterns or emotions. Fear can stop our momentum or advancement toward making a better life for ourselves if we become afraid of changing or breaking old habits. There are so many fears, such as fear of disappointment, failure, success, or rejection. I can go on and on. If you happen to experience failure, get back up and try another way of doing that thing you failed at. Learn from your mistakes. Failure often leads to success when you don't give up. Make a plan in advance to help you take action regarding different situations you may fear. Perhaps you fear trying new life experiences. Fear of public speaking is an example of a new life experience. The more you practice speaking in public, the more comfortable and confident you will become until you decrease your fear.

Thinking positive will also bring you into the light of love. The more you practice interrupting negative thoughts and letting go of negative feelings, the better you will feel. When you experience the need to make a choice related to any situation that offends you or is difficult, ask yourself this question: Does this situation or choice honor me or add value to my life? If it does not, then you should consider your reaction, voice, or self-transformation options toward the situation, until you are honored.

Think about anger, for example. Anger negatively affects the person delivering the anger, as well as the person receiving it. Anger is like drinking poison and hoping the person you are angry at gets ill. Anger creates negative energy in your body and soul and can cause disease due to the radical vibrations of your cells. This can also lead to other negative physiological effects on your body. Anger toward another person is negative energy. It is not peaceful energy. Does anger add value to your life? As I also mentioned before, my amazing, talented, and brilliant mother always told me, "She/he who angers you conquers you." I do not want to let anger shoot me down. Nor do I want anger to intimidate another person. Nobody is perfect; however, most people experience anger from time to time. I never forgot what my mother told me, so I wake up each day with the mind-set of choosing to be in good spirits. I admit this is much easier to say than do; therefore, practicing mindful workouts will help train you to be in control of your emotions. When a negative thought enters your mind, practice being aware of that thought and interrupt it. Switch your thought to something positive. Distract yourself to something positive around you to eliminate the negative thought. If someone angers you, let them know what they did. Confront them in a smart or professional way to try and interrupt their behavior and stand up for yourself, then let it go. When you learn to let go of issues that are bothering you, you conquer them. If you continue to let something bother you, it conquers you. The more you practice interrupting negative thinking or letting go of issues that are not value-added, the easier it will become to enjoy a better state of mind.

      The key to any daily or life challenge is to remember that the power of choice is in your control. You have the power to choose how you feel and how you react to any situation. You have the right to choose to honor yourself. If you have negative thoughts or feel powerless, it is up to you to seek professional assistance if you feel you need it. It is also important to learn to redirect your thoughts and practice mindful workouts. I named this "Mind Massage." Use it to strengthen and redirect how you think about yourself and your situations.

Mind Massage is anything you can do to relax, clear or redirect your thoughts for improved mental-emotional wellness. You would get a body massage if your muscles were aching, wouldn't you? Then why wouldn't you massage your mind to help transition it to a more peaceful state? Mind Massage includes anything that you feel comfortable doing to relax your mind, such as meditation, prayer, chanting, sitting in silence, dancing, singing, laughing, or using the affirmation statement "I am" (i.e., I am smart, I am beautiful, I am going to have an amazing day).

Hack Your Mind to Master Your Mind and Find Your Purpose:

Quick Mind-Hacks in Your Bare Feet:

- Wake up each day and set your thoughts into a positive and happy mind-set.
- Choose the best shoes to step into your successful day.
- Set or write down your goals for your day. Make a list of priorities to keep you on task and minimize distractions.
- Use positive affirmation statements with "I am" to start your day and relate them to your daily or life goals. For example, say to yourself, "I am healthy, I am influential." Whatever you need to feel, state it on a regular basis and believe it!

Mind-Massage Exercises for Your Higher Heels:

- Use positive self-talk, meditation, prayer, exercise, relaxation, or visual imaging.
- Create a vision board with construction paper by pasting magazine or other images on it to remind you of your ultimate life goals for the year.
- When you start to have negative thoughts about a situation, interrupt them and turn them into positive or distracting thoughts. Eliminate the negative thought by going on a walk, exercising, calling a friend, writing in a journal, doing a craft, etc. Do not give yourself permission to think negatively. You must practice this to master this.
- Create boundaries, so you are prepared when others try to cross them.
- Minimize or eliminate negative, judgmental, or abusive people from your life.
- When you feel confused or disturbed about something, take a pause and go change your shoes. Find a mentor, a counselor or other support person or persons to call when you need support.
- Practice the same things that work for you during the day before you go to bed (prayer, meditation, etc.).

Master Your Mind to Find Your Purpose:

In addition to your Mind Massage exercises, I recommend making a plan to take actions that will improve your life. Again, if you regularly feel sad due to your situation or feel depressed, I recommend you seek the advice of a physician or medical professional. You may have a chemical or hormonal imbalance that needs attention; or you just need to find guidance to change your situation.

- Create a goal or goals related to your strengths and talents. Follow your heart!
- Develop action strategies to support your goals for whatever you want accomplish
- Develop timelines to keep you on the right path and will lead you toward your goals
- Hold yourself accountable. If you fail, change your shoes again, get back up, adjust your strategies and never quit.
- Find a support person(s) to help cheer you on
- Make the choice to give thanks for any and all good things every day.
- Dr. Mo's resources: Free podcasts, take my courses and workshops https://www.HighHeelFootprint.com

Remember that choosing to start your day with a good attitude will motivate you to influence others. Be a role model and walk into your blessings. There will always be different life situations and people that can affect us in a negative manner; however, the choice is absolutely up to us as to how we choose to feel and react. Strive to be in control of your emotions. If you choose emotions such as anger, or unhappiness, it can consume you. Practice letting go of negative feelings and frustrations that do not add value to your life to find your peace. It is very easy to let yourself spiral downward into a depressing state of mind. Feelings of worry are very unhealthy for your total well-being. It can lead to disease. The challenge is to become encouraged and motivated to take charge and get yourself out of your rut by shifting your mind-set. Make changes, not excuses. Choose to live by choice, not by chance. Choose self-esteem and not self-pity. Learning to control the choices in your life is very important. Focus on understanding and changing the way you think of a situation to help you feel better.

Successful Relationships

We all know the struggles of aspiring toward successful relationships. If you are one of the lucky people in a successful

relationship, I salute you! I bet there are more of you out there with unhappy relationships. Here is a big tip: Although I cannot help you find the perfect partner, friend or relative, if you are longing for a happy and loving relationship of any kind, you must first love yourself.

Characteristics of a healthy relationship include mutual respect, trust, honesty, communication, support/lifting each other up, fun, and sharing quality time. Toxic relationships include criticism/judgment; lack of compassion, communication, or respect; substance abuse; control/power; sneakiness and hidden agendas; physical, sexual, or mental abuse; aggression; excessive jealousy due to distrust; inability to let go of past relationships to move forward; or cheating (emotionally or physically). If you find yourself in a toxic relationship, get help, counseling or get away.

Tips for a Healthy Relationship (partner, friend, relative)

- If a person is interested in you, they will pursue you. You could choose to reciprocate if the feeling is mutual.
- If a person doesn't call right away, be patient and give them some time. They may be busy with work or other commitments. Once they call, reciprocate and express your intentions and expectations so you can both be clear.

- A healthy relationship does not have secrets. If there are people or things to hide in each other's lives, then your relationship may suffer. Good relationships have good communication and are honest. Secrets will create distrust and can lead to a failed relationship. Consider one's character. Character can be defined by the action one takes when no one is looking. People with poor character try to get away with things that are deceptive and not honorable.
- When you are ready and feel comfortable with the timeline you choose in a relationship, introduce family members or old friends (male or female) to your partner/friend to observe and confirm they establish trust and inclusion. If you wait too long, however, or choose not to introduce them to others in your circle, it would be disrespectful to not include them in your life, and perhaps you should not be hiding this person or in a relationship with them. That is not fair either.
- Support your partner, friend, relative and lift them up. Compliment them. Have fun conversations about their day or their projects. Be interested. Ask how you can best help them.

- If a couple, human touch and intimacy can bring you closer together. Having trusting conversations can help alleviate stress.
- If you find yourself in a toxic or violent relationship, talk about it with a counselor, or other trusted person to open your eyes. You may need to be alerted to realize the toxicity, so you can move on. Breaking up with a partner, friend or family member is hard to do, but consider the alternative of being miserable and unhappy—Love yourself first! Detox or end a bad relationship because you are worth it!
- Have fun! Go on regular dates. Exercise, laugh, love, and share life!

Boundaries

Learning to create boundaries is important to the evolution of your personal development. It is healthy to have clear boundaries. Boundaries are guidelines or limits you set between you and other people, which determine what thoughts, activities, or behaviors are safe, honorable and permissible to you. Set them according to your best interest. Boundaries can be physical, sexual, spiritual, relational, emotional, mental, or legal. The challenge in creating boundaries lies in not wanting to hurt someone else's feelings, but running the risk that they will continue to hurt yours. Did you know the shortest route to better boundaries is to really like yourself? Better yet, really love yourself.

Learning to establish boundaries is very important for your mental health and self-esteem. If you do not learn to create boundaries and let go of your guilt, then people will most likely take advantage of you. Can you think of situations in your life where you should have had boundaries with others? Ask yourself how you really want to be treated. Understand your true feelings, and make yourself a priority over an uncomfortable request.

When you have boundaries, it becomes value-added to your life. Learning to have boundaries increases your self-esteem and the respect others have for you. When people try to control you or make you do something you are not comfortable with, your established boundaries will allow you to take charge of your reaction to their behavior or requests. Boundaries interrupt their negative behavior.

Learning to establish boundaries comes with a warning . . . This is usually not easy because people who are controlling or demanding have been used to always getting their way. A change in your reaction will most likely upset the pattern of your interactions with that person for better or worse. Sensitive strategies to start creating boundaries include being direct, and kind and always professional. As there are several types of situations or boundaries, I am only going to discuss a few examples.

Generic Example of a Key Problem

You have a partner, friend, family member who seems to constantly cross your boundaries. You are a caring person, and you do not want to make them feel bad or cause any waves, so you tolerate their behavior toward you.

How to Create Boundaries

First, you need to understand your feelings and your limits. There should be no tolerance for intentional negative behavior or when an intent was to make you feel bad. Tell the person that you have some personal priorities you are working on for yourself and that you are going to start creating boundaries and limitations when people say or do things that make you feel uncomfortable.

As I said earlier, the consequences to you setting boundaries may cause them to get upset. It is okay and part of the process. They own their behavior. Let it go because it is not your behavior. Instead, focus on yourself and do not argue with them. It may take several tries to practice setting your boundaries and creating solutions to break the pattern together before you see results. Practice, practice, practice!

Two key steps to try to break and change the pattern

Step #1: When a person crosses your boundary, let them know what they did and that their behavior is not okay with you. Tell them you are going to walk away or if you are on the telephone, tell them you are going to hang up or redirect your conversation elsewhere. This will cause the other person to stop and think about their behavior because it is no longer being ignored (even though they may get upset).

Step #2: When this person crosses your boundary again, remind them what they did. Ask them if they are willing to schedule a time to talk about what they did to cross your boundary. If you both have several habits, please only choose one to talk about at a time during one session. Once you schedule the time to talk, both of you can discuss the one thing that bothers each of you. Discuss the reactions and how they make each of you feel. Agree on solutions to interrupt the pattern, so you can both work together to improve the relationship. The truth is, without agreed-upon solutions, there will be no progress. The next steps may be to seek professional counseling or end the relationship as a last resort. It will depend on how important your relationship is.

Other Examples

If your partner, friend or relative causes you to feel untrusting of them, bring up the situation. Tell them you would like to understand why they want to do what they do. Assess how you feel when this happens, and share your feelings with them. Address how they have broken your trust. Discuss how long this trust has been broken. Is their action repetitive despite your requests? If so, make a request to compromise their behavior, and ask them for solutions that move toward increasing your trust. If they refuse, then set your boundaries or take action in whatever way you feel you need to for the relationship. If there is no motivation to make a change, you have the right to reevaluate the relationship to determine if it adds value to your life or not.

Exercise on "How to respond to someone overstepping your boundaries"

- How to say "no" to extra requests for commitments or volunteering:
  - *Although this organization or company is important to me, I need to decline your request to volunteer because I have other personal or family priorities at this time.*
- How to set boundaries with someone who borrows money:
  - *I love you and I hope you can learn to take responsibility for yourself; therefore, I will not be lending you money in the future.*
- How to set boundaries with angry people"
  - *I do not appreciate your anger. You may not yell at me, and if you continue, I will leave the room (or hang up the phone), or separate myself from your life.*
- How to set boundaries with people who are judgmental:
  - *It is not okay for you to comment about me that way. I would like for you to stop.*
- How to set boundaries when someone is pushing you into a sale or other decision:

- *I don't feel comfortable making quick decisions. I will think about it over the next day or so and get back to you.*

Your Turn: Think of your own situations with people you need to create boundaries with. Create a plan.

> A.) Who is the person you would like to create a boundary with?
>
> B.) What is the situation or patterned behavior that needs to be interrupted? (for both of you).
>
> C.) How will you confront this person and what will your conversation be? What is your ask?
>
> D.) What are you going to do to interrupt the behavior? Is it agreed upon?
>
> E.) What are you going to do if the behavior continues? Do you have a timeline?

The most important thing you need to do to set boundaries is to first stop ignoring what bothers you. When you ignore bad behavior, it does not go away. When you set your boundaries, do not feel obligated to defend or debate your feelings. Try to overcome your fear of setting your boundaries by practicing what you will say the next time something happens. Stay committed to your self-respect and goals. Be direct, but remain as pleasant as you can to disrupt their behavior as well as your usual reaction (this is also part of your ownership of the problem). If you do not stay strong and practice, you will continue to allow others to cross your boundaries. It is important for you to break the patterns of inappropriate behaviors that are not in your best interest.

Understand your emotions and try to be in control of them. I recommend you schedule a time to talk with the other person about your boundaries. Once you schedule this time, set discussion parameters and expectations. Be polite but firm. Avoid negative body language like rolling your eyes or talking back. Do not get angry or argue. If your confrontations get out of control, have a pre-made agreement to either stop, count to ten, take a timeout or walk away. Schedule another time to talk about your issue, so it gets resolved. Without addressing your issues, however, they will become stale and unresolved. This is unhealthy. Set your limits and refuse to engage with people who do not respect your boundaries. Talk about the changes you would both like to make in the relationship. Identify fears and solutions to overcoming them. Remember that each change may not be set mutually, so it is okay to be somewhat flexible. If agreements are made, keep practicing using your boundaries until the negative cycle is broken. You can do it!

Create a Vision Board for Goal Setting and Inspiration

A vision board can be a fun, helpful reminder of what your goals and desires are for the year.

To create a vision board, you will need:
- any color of cardstock or bulletin board paper,
- scissors,
- a glue stick or glue,
- magazines or images relating to your goals/vision, and
- optional art supplies, such as markers, crayons, glitter, or fun stickers.

Once you have your supplies, you can either do this alone or invite a group of friends over for a vision board party. Cut out vision images that depict your goals from magazines or print them from the internet. For example, if your goal is to have zero debt and more income, find a photo of a pile of money. If your goal is to graduate college, find a photo of a degree or students at a

graduation. Write your name on the degree with a date. If another goal is to get married, find a picture of a wedding ring. Add photos of yourself to your vision board. Paste everything onto a cardstock or bulletin board. Be creative, write positive statements next to your pictures, then decorate it with glitter, other colors, or artwork. Display your vision board anywhere you will see it daily. Meditate or pray to visualize your life in the state of your successful goals. Let it remind you of your vision/goals to keep you on track with your plans. Enjoy!

Monitor and Master Your Finances

Do you know what you spend your money on? Do you know the balance of your income versus your expenses? Do you have enough money saved to afford a comfortable life for such items as a vehicle, home, utilities, food, clothes, travel, or other things? The ability to monitor your finances is also an important item to consider when creating a balanced and healthy life. If not already doing so, create a monthly Excel file (or use other software or paper visual document) that includes your income and expenses for each month. Plan all future payment schedules for your monthly bills and credit cards until they are paid off. As your situation or income changes each month you may have unexpected expenses. It is okay. All you need to do is adjust your payments for the month, then resume your normal payoff plans or modify the plan to fit your ability to pay.

Cut back on spending. Find an area you can afford to cut back on, such as socializing, eating out, entertainment, or frequent shopping for items you want but do not need. I taught my children early about the difference between items they want and items they need. It helps to make better purchasing decisions. Monitor everything and be sure to set aside money for savings, retirement, and unexpected expenses. One common concern is that people think they cannot afford to set aside money. Choose an amount that is comfortable for you right now depending on your income. Even if you make minimum wage, you should set aside 10 percent or anywhere from $20 to $100 per paycheck. If you make a larger salary, you should set aside a minimum of 10 to 20 percent in a savings account each pay period. If you can afford to save more, that is even better! Have it automatically deposited into a savings or retirement account each pay period. You really need to pay yourself first. There is no better time to start than right now. If you are unsure how to do this, ask a friend or family member whom you trust to help you. Your local banking institution usually has

financial advisors available to consult with, and there are also numerous financial advising companies.

Mentoring or Coaching

Find a mentor, or two or more. Lack of feeling supported can often lead to feeling depressed, disappointed, or stressed. A network of mentors, including people in your personal circle of family, friends, place of worship or community group is just as important as finding professional coach or mentors at work or in your line of business. Ask someone you admire, trust, or honor to be your mentor or coach. Meet with them or call them on an agreed-upon schedule. Discuss your goals and strategies regularly. Ask for advice or resources related to your career, business, or personal life. Allow them to guide you. Find more than one mentor, because each person will be able to help you with their unique talents and expertise related to different issues.

Become a mentor or coach. There are several community organizations that are always recruiting mentors. Be a mentor to someone in your organization or establish a mentoring program. Utilize and share your knowledge, and expertise to guide and assist someone else. Pay it forward. Mentoring can be very rewarding. Mentoring is like planting seeds and watching them grow.

Examples of mentoring may include guiding someone with their education plan, career plan, relationships, or projects.

Practice Mind Massage

Lack of self-care can often lead to feeling unhealthy both mentally and physically. Your thought patterns affect your mental/emotional health. As a reminder, I created the term Mind Massage to relate to anything you can do to relax, clear, or redirect your thoughts. Mind Massage must be practiced on a regular basis to maintain a healthy thought pattern.

> Can you think of some strategies to help set you into a positive mindset as you wake up each day?
>
> Can you decide what your best shoes will be for whatever your day has in store?

If you practice Mind Massage exercises every day, you will become stronger and wiser. You will train yourself to let go of worry and be in control of your thoughts, thereby affecting your attitude. Having a good attitude will motivate you to influence others, be a role model, and walk into your blessings. Every day is a new chance to turn things around. Put your best foot forward and choose to leave amazing footprints as you walk up the path that contributes to a happy, healthy, and successful you. Make a positive influence in your world! Once you get to a healthy place of mind, your soul will radiate optimism. You will attract people who need your help, as well as people who will enter your life to help you.

Once you make Mind Massage a regular mental exercise and daily habit, you will be ready to take action toward your life purpose and fulfillment. Decide on the changes you want to make in your life. Set your goal(s). Take action toward your strategies. Be clear about what do you need to do to achieve a healthy, happy, balanced life.

Goal Setting

Finding your purpose and your High-Heel Footprint requires you to take action to make better choices, identify and adhere to your values. You are also required to make a commitment to yourself in efforts to set sturdy goals. Doing so will increase your sensibilities and awareness of the perceptions of others. Without commitment, you will most likely fail. Learning to create strong boundaries will help you transform your life. Setting goals involves identifying one or more things you want to accomplish in your day or life. Goals can be set for daily, weekly, monthly, quarterly, or annual achievements. For example, if you want to create daily goals, I recommend that you create a priority list of tasks for your day. Work on the harder task first to get it over with, and then work on completing the smaller tasks for a winning day. If you are interested in creating a large goal, such as writing a book or starting a business, your goal can be broken down into smaller objectives with timelines or deadlines for you to tackle. This makes your larger goals easier to achieve. Please do not be too hard on yourself if you do not achieve your goals. You must have self-love and compassion for yourself. Contact me to send you the High-Heel Playbook for a full goal-setting plan. The Playbook is age appropriate and I created one for Women, one for Girls (Jr. high +), and at the request of my two sons, I created a Playbook for Guys (big boots only, sorry no high-heels involved).

Goal setting requires you to identify something you would like to accomplish. Ask yourself to identify strategies and a timeline to achieve your goal. Figure out if you need help. Create a plan of how you can do better as a result of not achieving your goal

the first time. Address any challenges or obstacles and try again. Minimize or eliminate any distractions. If reality does not allow you to find the time to focus on your goals, then you will most likely fail. Wanting something and not taking action is, unfortunately, the downfall of most people who cannot commit to themselves. These are the people who continue to complain about their life and blame others, while they don't seem to take responsibility for taking the time to focus on making their own life better. Take the next steps by completing the goal-setting matrix found on the following page. What shoes will you need to step into?

Goal-Setting Exercise: For school, career, health, relationships, finances, or life balance:

List 3 realistic goals:		
1.	2.	3.
List any challenges or obstacles to achieving your goals:		
1.	2.	3.
List 3 things you can do to take action to overcome your challenges or obstacles and achieve your goals.		
1.	2.	3.
Make a commitment to yourself: Signature: _____ Set Goal Achievement Date: _____ List a support person (or persons) who you will ask to follow up with you daily or weekly:		

Share Your Story

Think about your personal story. Everyone has a story. The importance of sharing yours is to help others who may also have experienced the same thing as you. When we find out that someone else has had the same or similar life experience, it makes us feel as though we are not alone.

Sharing also demonstrates love, acceptance and trust, which are all worth spreading around. Learning how to cope or finding strategies to overcome a bad experience can help us evolve. Learning how others have achieved success can also help us evolve, and so can asking for help.

1. What have you experienced in your life that was a challenge or a success?

2. What did you do about it?

___ Nothing   ___Something I can share

3. How might you amplify this experience as a success story (to help you or someone else who may have had a similar experience)? If your experience was a challenge, how did you, or will you make it a success story?

84

Simple Steps to Create a Value-Added Footprint:

- Wear your *authentic, preferred heels* to create growth and transformation in your life.
- Free yourself. Rise above to higher ground with *bigger/stronger heels* and higher expectations; be prepared to *walk forward* and believe in yourself.
- Examine your *heel choices and heel options* before making decisions; don't react immediately with bad intentions or stomping.
- Live up to your own expectations by modeling your leadership and *collaboration heels.*
- Wear your *courageous heels,* and act with confidence to think critically for yourself and not only about what others think.
- Nurture your body, mind, and spirit for *optimal heel health.*
- Eliminate the disease to please. Learn to say no when your *heels are hurting and you need a break.*
- Create *heel boundaries* for those who are offensive or take advantage of you. (Do not look the other way and pretend it's okay); a *light heel tap* may be in order.
- Interrupt your self-doubt by releasing your guilt, anger, fear, pain, and vulnerability; don't be controlled by *bad*

heel thoughts; don't remain silent; *heel therapy* may be a solution.
- Live life with a sense of daily *heeling gratitude*.
- Use *optimistic healing words*; avoid pessimism or inappropriate/offensive statements.
- Teach and share your *heel wisdom* with others; be a servant leader.
- Be *heel innovative* and shoe creative with your life. It can lead to something better.
- Interrupt and *change bad heel habits* by setting daily intended goals and acting on them to improve your life. Wake up and walk up with a reason.
- Depend on *your self-chosen heel* (not others') to make you happy and fill your life with meaning and purpose.
- Do not spend a lot of time investing in a heel that is not in sync with you or your goals. Walk out sooner than later if it's not working to *save a heel-load of wasted time.*
- Evolve based on what you learn from others' *good or bad heel experiences.*
- Learn to include *restful, relaxing, and fun heels* in your life.
- Shift your thoughts from fear-based heels to *love-based heels*.

Chapter 4: Strategies for Organizations To Evolve the High-Heel Footprint

It is important for the development of any organization to retain or amplify its diversity, inclusion and engagement initiatives. Employee resource groups (ERGs) are one way to support diversity and inclusion. Organizations can support the establishment of voluntary employee-led ERGs for women, different cultures, sexual orientations, human abilities, or other life experience needs. These groups can support the workforce, while also supporting an organization's mission. This chapter discusses ERGs in more detail later in this chapter. Effective organizational strategies can support the innovation and growth of an organization by retaining good employees who remain loyal to the company. Happy and valued employees want to remain in an organization. It is important for leadership to identify strategies to eliminate both intentional and unintentional bias to achieve retention and create an organizational culture shift toward being "one team."

Providing a unified voice for all women is evident. The advancement of women, however, becomes complicated when adding ethnicity, sexual orientation, and class to the mix. While the "glass ceiling" is referred to as the barrier for women in the general corporate arena, African American women and women of color experience the "concrete ceiling." This metaphor assumes that the barriers and biases toward their advancement in the workplace are even more difficult to penetrate due to the lack of visible assignments, mentoring, workforce development or other opportunities. The metaphorical term for Latinas is called the "sticky floor." This discriminatory employment bias keeps them in pink collar jobs or from recognition related to workplace advancement similar to other women of color. In efforts to make gains for all women in the workplace, including women of color, diversity and inclusion issues must be addressed in organizations as well as in society.

Differences among women must also be addressed in order to improve daily work practices. This includes improved communication, networking, respect, and accountability in the workplace. Micro-aggressions can be responsible for hindering the advancement of women in the workplace. Women must come together collectively to address and implement changes in organizational systems by challenging the current or dominant organizational culture. They should also support other women to make our workplaces better and more effective.

While more management opportunities exist today for women, some still remain at a distance from powerful corporate positions. According to the United States Department of Labor (www.bls.gov/ted/2017), only 39 percent of managers in 2015 were women. The shares of women and men were nearly equal among financial managers, property, real estate, and community association managers. Women made up less than 20 percent of construction managers (6.7 percent), architectural and engineering managers (7.4 percent), and industrial production managers (18.3 percent). Additionally, 27.9 percent of chief executives were women.

The United States Department of Labor (www.bls.gov/ted/2017) reports women's and men's median earnings vary by occupation. For example, personal financial advisors had the greatest percentage difference in median weekly earnings between women ($953) and men ($1,714), followed by insurance sales agents ($676 women; $1,166 men); physicians and surgeons ($1,476 women; $2,343 men); real estate brokers and sales agents ($780 women; $1,222 men); and securities, commodities, and financial services sales agents ($951 women; $1,458 men). (U.S. Department of Labor, 2017).

Stereotyping in the workplace contributes to biased perceptions based on gender, race, physical ability/disability, and age of employees. Discrimination affects wages, lack of respect in the workplace, and occupational position. Research from the US Department of Labor shows that wage inequity is pointedly related to gender discrimination in the workplace. Latina women continue to stay at the bottom of the labor market by earning the lowest wages in comparison to other people (U.S. Department of Labor, 2017). Gender discrimination and bias presumes that men are more experienced and more knowledgeable than women, or it just gives a free pass to men for no other reason. Earlier in American history it was called the "good-ol' boy network." Efforts to debunk this myth include examining women's capabilities as a step in the right direction toward eliminating the practice of stereotyping.

Both women and men can be a source of support for emotional and intellectual development for other women. Those who adapt and become motivated can achieve positive results and overcome barriers. As participants in society, women should build community and professional networks, participate in role modeling and mentoring, and help other women take leadership positions. It is more important, they be instrumental in empowering other women to set goals for their lives or serve as mentors.

Organizations can help by placing a high priority on programs for women and minorities with a vision for inclusion. Programs or training to initiate or support increased intercultural understanding would raise the consciousness of employers, managers, and other staff members. Women are an asset, capable of creating and sharing innovative ideas. They are good at envisioning the big picture and multi-tasking. They are supportive and collaborative thinkers. Flexible work hours, increased personal and vacation time, childcare assistance, and benefits can help alleviate burdens placed on them by employers. Having family-friendly workplaces creates better work environments, higher productivity, and higher profits.

The definition of success is subjective. Success is usually associated with what we achieve or accumulate. Success can be what we learn each day and how much we grow. Doors of opportunity will eventually open for women who work hard and continue to have a vision for their success. Enthusiasm and

determination can help guide the way. Humanity should strive for a world that values the contributions of all citizens and a society more sensitive to the demands of working families so everyone can evolve and feel supported.

CEO's, Managers and Human Resource Tools for Success:

Establish Performance Expectations

Focus on productivity rather than time in the office. Work and family responsibilities are growing for all employees. This may include eldercare, childcare, or other family issues. Establish work/life balance policies to support organizational development and attrition planning. It is recommended that supervisors meet regularly with their staff to understand the bigger picture. Assuring that performance expectations are met, while helping employees find balance will create happier and healthier employees. Happier employees create better companies.

Coordinated Workforce Development Programs

Comprehensive workforce development training programs, and educational incentives, such as textbook tuition or tuition support for professional development. Offering internal training programs or opportunities for the workforce to attend external training, advances workplace knowledge and performance. Organizations are encouraged to survey the workforce and its leadership to determine training gaps. Identify best practice models to share and implement for improved trainings. Most organizations

have subject matter experts on staff payrolls. Utilize these experts to conduct internal train-the-trainer sessions to save training budgets.

Flexible and Visible Assignments

Provide employees with opportunities for learning other jobs or work assignments. Cross assignments or rotations at the company can benefit an unhappy employee, as well as help an organization to retain a good employee. Offering a chance to rotate or learn a new assignment and new experiences is a chance for an employee to develop their skills. Other flexible work assignments may include working on or leading special project teams.

Mentoring and Coaching Programs

One cannot underestimate the power and importance of mentoring or coaching. Establish one-on-one or group programs. Mentoring and coaching helps employees eliminate barriers to success, while offering opportunities for growth and development. Mentoring and coaching are characterized by trust and mutual sharing. Mentors/coaches serve as role models or champions to support and guide mentees. They can also suggest the involvement in company projects or other opportunities for increased visibility.

I recommend using my Master Mind model, "High-Heel Playbook" or "Big-Boot Playbook" as tools for individual/group goal-setting. Establish a regular time to meet with a group to support each other through the goal-setting process. Establish strategies for success, timelines, assessments and a support team. E-mail me at HelloDrMo@gmail.com for more information.

Employee Resource Groups (ERGs)

ERGs are voluntary groups also known as Affinity Groups. Establishing a variety of ERGs at an organization helps employees to network with people of similar backgrounds. ERGs meet regularly. The first benefit of an ERG is to help employees better understand the onboarding and orientation of being part of a new organization. ERGs help an organization evolve a diverse and inclusive workplace. They engage talent innovation, implement workplace best practices, share innovative presentations, and foster the organization's mission. ERGs can support the workforce by creating a sense of company loyalty and belonging.

Leadership Development

Good leadership is a key component of successful organizations. Does the majority of your leadership include a male culture? Commit to a culture of diversity and inclusion by eliminating the glass ceiling. All companies should conduct an environmental scan to identify the women and their talents in the organization. Do the women at the top reflect your customers or other staff members? Ask yourself if you are using all employee strengths to benefit your organization. Perhaps you have an employee with amazing talents, knowledge, experience, or education who is unhappy doing something else. Find that employee and help assign them to the best place in your organization to utilize their strengths. It's a win-win! Offer leadership development training. Identify how many of your talented female employees are in leadership positions. If you have very few or none at all, create opportunities or training programs to help promote those with the qualifications to serve in those positions. Stop talking the talk and start showing proof of being accountable for eliminating that glass ceiling. All too often I see the male leadership pat themselves on the back for promoting one woman to the top. That is an okay first step, but more needs to be done to effect social and organizational change in the workplace for more women.

Chapter 5:
The Way Forward

Abraham Maslow was a psychologist who theorized that basic human needs are predicated on fulfilling priorities. He developed the theory of the hierarchy of needs that includes physiological, safety, love/belonging, self-esteem and self-actualization needs. Maslow's theory suggests that as one fulfills the basic needs in their order of priority, the person becomes more self-actualized and self-transcendent; meaning one becomes wiser and has the knowledge and intuition of how to address a variety of situations. If you are taking a class, workshop, reading this book, or any other self-help book, you are on your way to becoming more knowledgeable or even self-actualized. If you have moved your life up from simply having basic needs, you are now most likely focused on personal growth, self-fulfillment, and realizing your fullest potential.

Many challenges still exist for women related to culture, selfless guilt, and the socialization of young women in society. If you implement some of the suggestions in the High-Heel Footprint, however, you will be taking action for securing a better place in the world. If you are a man, reading this book, it is my hope that you can also benefit from the suggestions of the High-Heel Footprint. You also have free will to choose the shoes you step into each day. They may be of a different style, but you can find your best self and footprint within your own reflection. Do you sometimes feel as though you are lost in a time warp, unsure of what to do next? Have you felt powerless when being judged by others you cannot control? Resilience is the ability to adapt in the face of tragedy, trauma, adversity, hardship, and ongoing significant life stressors. If you are capable of choosing your shoes, you are capable of choosing your thoughts. This is your power. Nobody else defines you. Please consider being in control of every aspect of your life by choosing your present emotion as the gift of your happy and purposeful future. What you practice will grow stronger. If you practice setting boundaries, you will get better at it. If you practice kindness, complimenting others and positive self-talk, you will get better at it. If you practice meditation, exercise, and prayer, you will get better at it. If you practice being judgmental, it will also grow stronger (not recommended). Sometimes taking action can mean taking the high road (being patient or knowing when to be silent). Taking action can also allow you to alter your path or release bad habits when the same thing is not working to evolve or elevate your soul. This is what gives us the opportunity to find our greater purpose. Go ahead! Be courageous. Take the chance and step into a new path in your best shoes.

When making a choice, ask yourself, does this choice honor me or others? Does this choice add value to the situation? Choose the best shoe that inspires and empowers you to live life to the fullest! Declare your goal, step up and visualize your path, plot your course, eliminate obstacles, walk, and then run there. Sometimes we may fall or stumble. That is okay. Ask yourself what you learned from the fall. Lift yourself back up, shake off the dust, and put on a stronger pair of shoes. Stay open to alternative roads that may also get you to your goal. These alternate roads might be a blessing in disguise. Take a chance and go there. Ask others for help if you need it. Don't waste your time trying to change the opinion of others. Be sure you put on the most comfortable or appropriate shoe for all situations. Bring value, dignity, blessings, and good mental, emotional, and physical health

to your life. Dance, sing, and care for your higher self. Leave your best footprint, and share it with the world!

In conclusion, this woman-ifesto only discussed issues at the surface. There is so much more to say in-depth about most of the concepts or issues in this book. Each issue can be its own book. My highlights are intended to bring a comprehensive awareness and call to action to my readers related to the historical and current issues of women. Spread the message to organizations to step up their high-heel footprint and work together to create positive organizational change, inclusive of ideas and strategies from the workforce. The High-Heel Footprint workshops, online learning and my coaching/consulting practice aims to further teach these issues.

I wish you much success in your journey toward personal and professional development. Your success is definitive to whatever you want it to be. Please do not let anyone or any circumstance define who you are. You are the amazing person God or your deity made you to be. Continue to reach for the stars, find your happiness, and step into your greatness. Validate yourself. Define your high-heel footprint, and find your purpose. Much peace and love, Dr. Mo.

About the Author:

Mona Armijo (Dr. Mo) is Chief Inspiration Officer of Dr. Mo Strategy Consulting and Mind Lab. She is a leading expert on women's research and organizational development. She is an author, educator, consultant, speaker, and life coach. Her motto is "making a difference." She coined the terms Mind-Massage, and the High-Heel Footprint. Dr. Mo was a university professor and chair for doctoral students in the colleges of business and public health at Columbia Southern University. She also taught comprehensive health education and global women's health at Oxnard Community College in California as a preferred professor for eight years. She helps organizations with strategic planning and training and is a lean six-sigma trainer. Her diverse professional knowledge has allowed her to lead a variety of high-level assignments. She worked as a special project lead for the US

federal, state and county governments, and was CEO of R.J. Consulting, Disaster Preparedness USA and now Dr. Mo Strategy Consulting and Mind Lab. Dr. Mo was named Latina Changemaker of the Year in 2009 by Walden University for her work leading social change initiatives, and has been honored with several community achievement awards for her work related to organizational and community education. She believes that nothing is impossible if you have faith in God and yourself. She believes the universe is and was made by a higher power, and respects others who have their own beliefs and faith. She inspires others to identify their life purpose by transforming their visions and desires into achievable life goals. She is especially passionate about the development and empowerment of women and girls around the world. To learn more, please visit https://www.HighHeelFootprint.com or contact Dr. Mo at: HelloDrMo@gmail.com

References

Annenberg Classroom. Retrieved from http://annenbergclassroom.org

Armijo, R.J., (2009). *The Challenges of Latina Professionals Related to Family, Culture, Personal and Professional Life.* Doctoral Dissertation. Walden University

Foreman, Amanda., (2016). *The Ascent of Woman: A History of Women from the Apple to the Pill.* Documentary

Garcia, A.M., (1997). *Chicana feminist thought: The basic historical writings.* New York: Routledge

Garcia, G.G., (1998). *Fluid identities, adaptable lives: The impact of educational and career experiences on the identity development of five Latina corporate managers.* (Doctoral dissertation). The University of Texas at Austin, Austin, Texas. Retrieved from http:proquest.waldenu.edu

Gilligan, C., (1993). *In a different voice: Psychological theory and women's development.* Cambridge, Massachusetts: Harvard University Press

Moloi, V., (2013). Retrieved from www.africanunbound.org

National Center for Education Statistics (2018). Graduate degrees by gender, culture. Retrieved from http://www.nces.ed.gov

Richman, I.B., (1919). *The Spanish conquerors: Chronicles of America.* Toronto: Yale University Press

Ruether, R.R., and Keller, R.S., (1986). *Women and religion in America: Volume 3: 1900–1968.* San Francisco: Harper & Row

Sharma, A., (1987). *Women in world religions.* Albany: State University of New York Press

U.S. House of Representatives, (2018). History, art & archives. The Women's rights movement, 1848–1920. Retrieved from http://history.gov/Exhibitions-and-Publications/WIC/Historical-Essays/

U.S. Department of Labor, (2004). Highlights of women's earnings in 2003. Retrieved from http://www.dol.gov/wb

U.S. Department of Labor, (2005). Employment status of women and men in 2005. Retrieved from http://www.dol.gov/wb/

U.S. Department of Labor, (2005). Women in the labor force: A Databook. Retrieved from http://www.dol.gov/wb/

U.S. Department of Labor (2006). Monthly labor review: The economics daily. Retrieved from www.bls.gov/opub/ted/2006

U.S. Department of Labor (2016). The economics daily. Retrieved from www.bls.gov/opub/ted/2016

U.S. Department of Labor (2017). The economics daily. Retrieved from www.bls.gov/opub/ted/2017

Villanueva, M. A., (2002). Racialization and the Latina experience: Economic implications. *Feminist Economics, 8,* 145

www.ingramcontent.com/pod-product-compliance
Lightning Source LLC
LaVergne TN
LVHW021356080426
835508LV00020B/2299